Allen Houston stretching his stirrups behind the chutes, Pro Rodeo Cowboys Association, Scottsdale, Arizona, 1964

Pages 2–3: *Hora de comida* **(Chow time),** Willow Springs Ranch, Oracle, Arizona, 1966

Page 4: **Matthew Terence's glove,** Yuma, Arizona, 1984

Page 5: **Thurman Mays and Everett Brisendine,** Cowpunchers Reunion, Williams, Arizona, 1983

Left: **Roy Humble,** Arizona Rodeo Association (amateur), Casa Grande, Arizona, 1963

Following page: **Matt Martin,** High School Rodeo Finals, Douglas, Arizona, 1974

Rodeo

Photographs and Text by
Louise L. Serpa

Notes by

Larry McMurtry

An *APERTURE* Book
published by
KÖNEMANN

Ricky Stock, Pro Rodeo Cowboys
Association, Willcox, Arizona, 1984

Skeeter in the Dust, Roy "Skeeter" Humble riding bareback in a dust storm, Chandler Junior Rodeo, Arizona, 1964

Rodeo is fueled by adrenaline; it is geared by athletic ability and heart. The odds of winning are not high, and the pay is the lowest of any sport. Constant traveling, lack of sleep, and physical soreness make some men burn out early. Few can afford to go down the road full-time and make a living at it; those who can't are known as "weekend warriors"—men who hold regular jobs but ride in rodeos in their free time. For all of them, it holds a challenge, freedom, and camaraderie without par.

Rodeo is the great equalizer—there's no room for braggarts, bullies, or the fainthearted. No guts, no glory. It doesn't help to moan or complain—everyone has a tougher story to tell. It doesn't matter who you are, what you do for a living, how much money you have, or where you come from, as long as you're a regular person and can pull your own weight. As long as you have heart and try, and never take yourself too seriously, you can belong to the greatest fraternity imaginable.

As a photographer in the arena, my job is to record the action every time a chute gate opens—and *never* to get in the way. The worst thing for anyone working on the ground to do is interfere with the action: it's better to get run over—flattened—than to alter the movement of any animal. You soon learn where to be for the various events, and to keep an eye on the nearest fence to climb—in case you need to get out in a hurry.

There is a rodeo ethic: man against beast, man helping man. After thirty-five years being a part of it, I still get the adrenaline surge, feel the excitement, the warmth of old friendship; I still anticipate the action, and wonder if I can be in the right place at the right time with the camera focused. From the photographer's point of view, rodeo is never static: no two rides are ever the same, and there is no time for a lag in concentration. It gives me a real charge. There is always something *somewhere* happening in the arena. As I've been quoted as saying, "Never don't pay attention." Bad English, but good advice in rodeo.

Rodeo doesn't stop for weather—rain, sleet, snow, heat, or mud. I can remember only one performance that was canceled, and that was because there were flood waters so high that the stock trucks couldn't get to the arena. Another time, Roy "Skeeter" Humble rode in a dust storm that was so thick the timers couldn't see well enough to time the ride. The rodeo was stopped and everyone ran for shelter, to breathe and wait out the storm. Afterwards, Skeeter got a reride.

Previous pages: **Jim Roer,** Cowpunchers Reunion, Williams, Arizona, 1983

Left: **Kay Vamvoras,** Pro Rodeo Cowboys Association, Globe, Arizona, 1983

Rodeo animals—bulls and bucking horses—and the timed-event stock—calves and steers—are vital to any successful rodeo production. People in rodeo get exasperated with animal activists' accusations of abuse. The animals are *not* abused. They are kept, fed, groomed, hauled, doctored, and housed better than a lot of backyard pets. The stock is the lifeblood of the stock contractors, so the animals must be healthy and in good shape. If they are hurt or sick, they simply won't buck. As it is, the rough stock "works" for only eight seconds a performance, which is not a lot, considering the costs of feed, hauling, and veterinary checks.

A lot of horses buck naturally; nowadays, some are even being specially bred to buck. The animals are really athletes themselves, and each horse and each bull has its own way of moving, its individual pattern of behavior. A given animal will usually buck the same way every time the chute gate opens, and a cowboy who has ridden that animal before can give advice to the rider who next draws it, letting him know that the animal turns to the left, spins, kicks high, breaks stride, or anything else—again, the camaraderie among the men is remarkable.

Many horses buck for the sheer joy of it. Some are soured saddle horses that no one could get the buck out of, so they're brought to the rodeo arena to see what they'll do. Many of them will buck with or without the flank strap—an adjustable leather strap that is tightened around the waist of the animal. If the strap is pulled too tightly, the animal may well refuse to buck at all, or may just stall in the chute. If it's properly pulled, the flank strap just gooses the animal a bit, without inflicting pain—it's an annoyance that the horse bucks to get rid of.

The events fall into two categories: *rough stock* (bull riding, bareback, and saddle bronc), and *timed events* (team roping, calf roping, and steer wrestling—also known as "bulldogging"). In all events, the stock is drawn by number from a hat. There are two judges who draw the stock for every contestant; they do this in front of the rodeo secretary, who makes sure that no rider competes on the same stock twice in a row. It is the luck of the draw: with some horses and bulls, no amount of riding talent and effort can make the rider mark high enough to win. In the timed events, how straight or how fast the animals run can make the difference—by seconds—that will mean a win or a loss.

All bareback and bull riders wear leather gloves on their riding hand, left or right. Both the glove and the bareback rigging (which looks something like a suitcase handle) have rosin rubbed into the leather, making it easier for the rider to keep his hand in the rigging.

In bull riding, the rider's only connection to the bull is a braided rawhide rope with a loop at one end. Another man will pull the rope tight over the rider's open hand, and then back across his palm, so that when the rider makes a fist the tension is kept. Often, he will pound on that fist with his free hand to reinforce the bond of the rosin on the glove and rope. If the bull's strength and drive force that hand to open, the rope comes loose and the rider falls.

The only points of contact to the horse in bareback riding are the man's hand in the rigging, and his backside. His legs should move with the action of the horse—forward when the horse drops its head, and raked back as the horse rears—and his free hand is used to keep his balance. If the free hand touches the horse at any time during the eight-second ride, the rider is disqualified. The judges give a lot of weight to the way a man uses his horse: his leg action (or "lick"), his balance, and whether he seems to make the horse buck harder. There are two judges, and each has fifty points to award: twenty-five for the way the animal bucks (which is what determines the difficulty of the ride), and another twenty-five for the man's actual ride. A good conglomerate score is in the eighties; ninety and over is exceptional.

For bull riding, the scoring works the same way, but the riding technique is different. Here, once the man has the rope in his clenched fist, he slides forward on the bull until his hand is tight against his crotch, legs flexed, toes turned out, free hand up. He then nods for the chute gate to open. The action of the bull is very different from that of the horse: the hide is so movable on the bull's frame that the rider must keep his legs tightly gripped to maintain his equilibrium and stay on top of the animal. If he works with the rhythm and spurs a bit, it may add to his score, but he risks being thrown before the whistle blows.

Saddle-bronc riding is a different story again. Each cowboy owns his own rig, called an "association saddle"—which is basically built like a Western saddle, but without the horn. The stirrups and the seat are custom fit to the rider. The horse has a halter with a buck rein—a heavy rope—attached, which the rider can hold in either hand.

Here, the balance and weight are distributed between the cowboy's backside—as tight as possible in the saddle— and his feet in the stirrups. If the rider's grip on the buck rein is too short, the horse will pull him forward over its head; if it is too long, he will go "out the back door" (off the back end). The proper grip is essential to a good ride.

In the horse rough-stock events—bareback and saddle-bronc—there is a judge on either side of the chute to check that the cowboy "marks" the horse out. This means that the bareback and saddle-bronc rider's heels must be in the points of the horse's shoulders when the chute gate opens and the timer starts. If they are not—if even one foot is missing the horse's shoulder—the yellow penalty flags will fly and the judges will simply stop watching; the rider is instantly disqualified.

One event that really shows the sportsmanship in rodeo is steer wrestling. The man who is wrestling the steer comes back in and "hazes" for the man who helped him on his run. "Hazing" means herding the steer in close to the wrestler himself. The steer comes out of the chute between two horses. And the man on the steer's right—the hazer—keeps the animal in tight, so that the man who is jumping onto the steer from his horse will have a proper angle from which to jump. Hazing is an integral part of rodeo's timed events.

Steer wrestling is very exacting. In the picture called *Miscalculation,* you can see just how tough it is. The rider in it is driving straight for the ground. He has missed the left horn totally with his left arm, which should be behind the horn. And he's coming off the horse at probably thirty-five miles an hour—the arena is really very hard when you're moving at that speed. The hazer is out of the picture, having kept the steer in close before the jump—and he's done a good job. But that steer "sucked back," as we say, just a little bit. And that allowed the "dogger" (the bulldogger or steer wrestler) to miss this steer, which should be right in the crook of his arm.

People say, "Oh, how mean to the steer!" Mean to the steer? This is the worst thing in the world for knees on a human being (even though the human being chooses to do it), because you're down there stopping the steer with your legs out, going thirty-five miles an hour on rough ground. You can drive a horn into your body very easily if you miscalculate any of the above. And the steer weighs five or six hundred pounds.

Each steer has a running habit or pattern, just as the horses or the bulls do in bucking. The rodeo secretary posts a list on the gate of who had that steer the last time, so you can tell how far the rider went down the arena, what kind of time he made up, how tough he was to throw. Depending on the arena, a good time is under five seconds from the moment the dogger leaves the chute until the steer is down with all four legs out.

The wrestling does not hurt the steer. Most bulldoggers are big men—we're talking two hundred-plus pounds. You have to have that bulk to put the steer down. John W. Jones has been National Champion three times. His father was dogging when I first started shooting, in the sixties, and was a National Champion before him. At only 185 pounds, John is actually not a very stout person, but he makes up for it in athleticism and timing: he's able to get down on the steer, and then use the momentum of the animal and the speed at which it's traveling to tip it over. All of these guys have to be absolutely superb athletes and in wonderful shape.

Usually, bull riders are quite small. Long legs do not help you in that particular event—or in bareback, really. It's the point of gravity as much as physical stamina—guts and all the rest of it—that are involved. Saddle-bronc riders tend to be bigger men. You very seldom get riders who do all three rough-stock events. That's why Ty Murray, the current champion, is unique—and he ropes as well.

Chuck wagons are raced in heats, with four horses to a hitch. I think there are only two places that have chuck-wagon races: one of them is Cheyenne, and Calgary is the other. At Calgary, four wagons race at one time around the track. They are mostly thoroughbreds, and there are four to a team. These drivers are canny, shrewd, and very, very aggressive.

These days, wild-horse races are held at Prescott and Calgary. Each team consists of three men. The chute gates open simultaneously, the horses come out, and the men have to try to cinch the saddle around the animal. One of the men then mounts and rides—as best as he can—to the end of the arena, while the horse is doing its level best to dump him.

Doug Houston is Allen Houston's son—a second- or third-generation rodeo baby grown up. In the picture of him steer wrestling, you can see—once the animal is fairly stopped—where the arms are in relation to the horns, and how the cowboy twists the steer around to lay it flat, with all four legs out.

Allen Houston was one of the first people I photographed in Tucson's pro rodeo who got into a real storm in saddle-bronc riding. His horse reared up in the chute, and went over backwards on him. This is why the so-called association saddle does not have a horn on it. If his saddle had had a horn, Allen would have suffered severe internal injuries—that horn would just about disembowel you. I was standing out in front of the chute, taking a picture. As I saw this happening, I dropped the camera. I was so worried about him being killed that I didn't think to snap the shutter. Allen called me from the hospital later that night, and he said, "Did you get the picture?" I said, "No, I was too worried about you." "Fat lot of good that does me," he said. "I wanted to see what happened—what I lived through!"

Team roping is exactly what the name implies: a team of two men (known as a "header" and a "heeler") working to rope a steer. But there is also precise teamwork between these men and their horses. Each run involves absolute trust, athleticism, instinct, and instant reflex, all within six seconds, which is considered a good time for the event. Team roping and calf roping are still used on roundups on the open range; out where there are no cattle pens or chutes, roping is a necessity for branding or doctoring animals with a minimum of trauma and stress to them.

The team that has been World Champions for a record six times is Clay O'Brian Cooper (whom I knew as a junior-rodeo roper) and Jake Barnes. Some time ago, they split up for a year—each one was roping with another partner. I'm very glad to see them back together, because they really make a wonderful team. When two men work together that closely, each has to be in sync with the other—they have to know and understand each other very well.

In the arena, the team-roping time starts when the header (the man who ropes the steer's horns) leaves the roping chute and throws a loop around the animal's horns, "dallies" (loops the saddle horn), and then moves off to his left. Meanwhile, his partner, the heeler (who ropes the animal's heels), comes up behind and lays what is called a "trap"—a loop across the back legs of the steer. The header's forward motion pulls the steer into the trap and instantly the heeler jerks the rope's slack, trapping both hind feet. Heeling is the one action in rodeo that happens so fast I actually have to push the camera's shutter before I see it take place; if I wait, it will be too late. With this split-second timing, the slack is pulled, the rope is dallied, the header turns and faces the steer, and the flag is dropped as the steer is "stretched."

Pages 22–23: **Wild horse race,** Prescott, Arizona, 1984

Douglas Houston steer wrestling, Pro Rodeo Cowboys Association, Tucson, Arizona, 1991

Below: **Carter Rogerson** in a
"long reach" for his steer, Pro Rodeo
Cowboys Association, Sonoita,
Arizona, 1991

In the picture of Kim Roberts steer wrestling, he's got his
left hand on one horn, and his right arm is going around
behind the other horn; his left leg is kicked loose and will
come down and meet the ground to stop the steer. The
horse is trained, after the rider drops, to peel off a little
bit to the left, leaving the dogger to stop and twist the
steer down. On rare occasions, the rider gets "hung up":
his foot goes through the stirrup, and the horse pulls him
off the steer again and just keeps going—dragging the
man until his boot comes off.

I watched a man get killed that way, right in front of
me, in Yuma. It's horrifying to see the horse dragging the
rider, right there, and not to be able to do anything about
it. He was dead before he got to the end of the arena,
because he went right under the horse, and the horse
just pummeled him to death in a panic. I saw the same
thing happen recently in Sonoita, but fortunately, the
rider's boot came off. The boot went right through the
stirrup, but the boot came off his foot—so he was banged
up, but he was alive. The horse was so panicked by this
whole thing happening underneath him that he tried to
jump the end of the arena. The horse was all right, but it
could have finished the rider.

Right: **Kim Roberts steer wrestling,**
Pro Rodeo Cowboys Association,
Tucson, Arizona, 1985

Page 28, top: **Marvin Hudson** "heading" steer for his father Jim Hudson, team roping, Pro Rodeo Cowboys Association, Willcox, Arizona, 1982; bottom: **Roy Cooper** "heading" as Ed Gaylord lays a heel loop, Pro Rodeo Cowboys Association, Tucson, Arizona, 1985

Page 29: **Travis Howe** untaping his glove, Turquoise Circuit Finals, Tucson, Arizona, 1993

Pages 30–31: **Brian Lopresto** calf roping, Pro Rodeo Cowboys Association, Willcox, Arizona, 1993

Today's rodeo is very much a competition of real athletes. They don't have nearly as much fun as we used to have! They're in training all the time. They don't go out drinking, smoking, partying, and misbehaving—they don't have the time. They keep better hours, and they have to keep in top physical shape. Some are getting over injuries, and so they have to do their therapy and their stretching. This rider is stretching the groin muscles and the hamstrings as well. Limbering up before you get on is important in order to make any kind of a decent ride. The clowns (or bullfighters) do the same thing, because they have to be fast on their feet in order to save bull riders who get in trouble and are hung up, or if a bull turns around and starts to charge. They really have to be on the go, and physically able the entire time. Warming up and keeping supple are essential.

Rodeos are stocked by licensed stock contractors, who are hired by hard-working and savvy local committees. There used to be just three or four important contractors in the whole United States; now there are over twenty for pro rodeo alone. The contractors own all the rough stock, and they will usually "job out" or lease the calves and the steers for the timed events from a subcontractor. Good stock is what makes a rodeo—it's what draws good cowboys.

Left: **Riders limbering up and stretching out,** Turquoise Circuit Finals, Tucson, Arizona, 1993

33

Lynn Beutler is the dean of stock producers. He's in his late eighties, and has basically turned over his empire of stock to his nephew Bennie. Lynn has always been a great gentleman, and a real connoisseur of good horse-flesh and bulls. Sonny Linger worked for years for Lynn as his livestock and chute boss. He was very knowledge-able about the bucking stock out in the arena; he went on to have his own string of horses and rough stock in Wyoming. Lynn's still alive, but not in terribly good health now. It will be a sad thing for rodeo when he leaves, because he is truly a legend.

Sonny Linger and Lynn Beutler (on horseback),
Pro Rodeo Cowboys Association, Phoenix, Arizona, 1965

One of the first sequences I ever shot was of Jim Mihalek riding Hud. I didn't have a motor-drive on the camera in those days, but with the hand-held camera, I could do five pictures in an eight-second ride without too much blurring from advancing the shutter manually.

Jim *rode* that horse; he didn't get thrown. The sad and ironic thing is that he failed to mark the horse out of the chute—he didn't have his feet up. He had a fantastic ride, which everybody knows, but he didn't get a marking on it because of that rule infraction.

These pictures show how athletic both the man and the beast have to be to survive in action like this.

One thing you're not supposed to do now in pro rodeo (in fact you get fined for it), is tie yourself onto the horse. In bareback, the fingers of your riding glove can be a little bit longer than your own fingers. Even if the glove fits properly on your hand, you can have extended fingers of the leather. And once you put your hand in the rigging, you tuck that extension back inside for the grip. So in effect, you are tying yourself onto the rigging. If you get bucked off, and your hand doesn't come loose, you're in deep trouble. That's where your "pick-up men" come in, the men who ride out and get the contestants safely off the animals. They are real lifesavers. They take the man off the bucking horse: when the ride is through, if he hasn't been bucked off, they will ride on either side of the bucking horse, loosen the flank strap, and give the man a lift off without his having to hit the deck. And also, if the cowboy gets hung up on the horse, the pick-up man is the one who must try to stop the horse, while going "down in the well" (between the other man's horse and his own) to get his hand loose.

Above: **Jim Mihalek** riding the Beutler brothers' horse Hud (second jump),
Pro Rodeo Cowboys Association, Tucson, Arizona, 1971

Right: **Jim Mihalek** riding Hud.
The same ride, fifth jump.
Pro Rodeo Cowboys Association, Tucson, Arizona, 1971

Junior rodeo (where I started in 1960, with my Argus
C3 twenty-seven-dollar camera) has launched most of
the stars of the pro-rodeo circuit. The two junior associa-
tions, Little Britches and the Arizona Junior Rodeo
Association (AJRA), are wonderful proving grounds.
Junior rodeo is divided into three age groups: five to
twelve, thirteen to fifteen, and sixteen to eighteen. Most
of the kids who compete come from second- and third-
generation rodeo families. They get hooked on the sport
when they're young. Junior rodeo is very family oriented—
fathers and mothers rope with their kids; teach them to
ride; camp out with them at the arenas; coach them;
cheer them on; and form close friendships over the years.

In the early sixties, I was on the founding board of
the AJRA. At that time, the stock was uneven in quality,
and the judging had some problems. So a group of
parents and other concerned people formed the organization, complete with a rule book, in order to give kids a
fair shake.

High-school rodeo is the next step, and has its own
association, which is very strong, and also runs a National
Finals competition. After that comes the college-level
rodeo, organized by the National Intercollegiate Rodeo
Association (NIRA). Some colleges are now offering
scholarships to rodeo competitors.

In all these categories of rodeo competition, young
people learn a kind of sportsmanship that is found in no
other sport. Many of the kids go from college right into
pro rodeo (after they have won $2,500 in competition—
a requirement to qualify for a permit in the Pro Rodeo
Cowboys Association, or PRCA).

When I first got my "pro card," which allows me to
shoot in any professional arena, there was maybe one
rodeo per week happening in the whole country. Nowadays, on some weekends, there can be as many as ten
rodeos. And this is why the "circuit system" was developed.
Now, with six thousand cardholders, plus the permit hold-
ers, twelve circuits are needed to manage the small
rodeos. With this system, there are now about eight hundred rodeos per year, which culminate in the National
Circuit Finals. Rodeo has become an enormous business.

Twila Hamman barrel racing,
Arizona Junior Rodeo Association,
Globe, Arizona, 1968

In professional rodeo, barrel racing is the only event in which women compete. It involves running a horse around three barrels, set in a cloverleaf pattern, against a split-second clock. There is a women's rodeo association, which sanctions all events—including rough stock—for women; and in amateur rodeo, women team-ropers ride, and are highly competent.

These days, most rodeos have what is known as "slack." It is essentially for the timed-event contestants. Slack is judged competition that is run before the audience-attended performances take place. At the Tucson rodeo, for instance, there are so many entries for the timed events that, in order for them all to have a chance, they run a "go-round" before the performances. Monday morning at sunup, all the entered ropers, steer wrestlers, and barrel racers will compete, just once. The next day, the contestants with the slower times start a second go-round, and the rest of the riders—about ten in each event, per performance—compete in front of the general public. The winnings are paid to the cowboys with the top times for each "go," and also to the best average times for all the go-rounds.

Now, with so many contestants at rodeos, everything is organized by computer ahead of time, so riders can enter four or five rodeos a weekend. And many of the top hands do, over the Fourth of July, which has been dubbed "Cowboy Christmas." A man competes in his event, then races to the airport to catch a plane to the next rodeo—some of them even own or rent their own planes. But you can't fly your horses, so the timed-event men have a driver haul their animals to the specific rodeo, or trade off horses trained in their events, and then they fly in to compete. If one man wins on another man's horse, he pays a percentage of his winnings to the owner. Rough-stock riders just get on the plane and go, and hope they get there on time. All their stock is drawn for them before they get there, according to performance, and they try to synchronize it with the other rodeos they're competing in.

Top: **Yates Dixon** riding his first calf at the Cowpunchers' Reunion, Williams, Arizona, 1983

Bottom: **David Motes** "heeling" for his father Glen Motes, Arizona Junior Rodeo, Mesa, Arizona, 1964
David has been a Pro Rodeo Cowboys Association National Finalist eleven times.

Right: **Aftermath,** examination of Cole Gould's wound after his calf ride, Cowpunchers' Reunion,
Williams, Arizona, 1983

Above: **Pat Kirby riding Dew Britches,** Pro Rodeo Cowboys Association, Yuma, Arizona, 1983
Right: **Gerald Farr on Widow Maker,** Arizona Rodeo Association, Ajo, Arizona, 1963

The pictures of Pat Kirby riding Dew Britches give you some idea of what the rider has to do. He is giving the horse a "lick," as they call it—traveling with his feet from the horse's shoulders back with his spurs. It doesn't hurt the horse a bit, but it makes the rider look better, so he scores higher, as he's "giving some action" to the horse. Each person has a different style. Some people find that if they almost lie back on the horse's back, they can do more with their legs; a lot of others sit forward. Each has his style, just as each horse has its own style of bucking. The competition is in using the horse, making it buck as much as you possibly can, while at the same time getting the best style yourself. It's a whole combination of things. There is no predictability about any of it—that's what's so exciting. You never know what's going to happen, not the person on the ground taking the pictures, not the person who is riding. So you never sink back and think, "Oh, yawn, here we go again"—because it's not ever the same. Every time presents a new challenge.

Widow Maker reared every single time she came out of the chute: she always went up, but I never saw her go over backwards. If you look at Gerald Farr's legs in the picture of her, you see they are where they belong, despite the fact that he is literally hanging right straight up vertically. Once the horse finally got out of the chute, she didn't buck all that hard, so the cowboys learned to hate her, because you couldn't mark very high on her.

There's a picture here of Lewis Feild's butt—and it's a very famous butt. He's behind his saddle bronc at Yuma. Lewis was All-Around Champion of the World for three years, I believe. Lewis's mother-in-law is one of the best female rodeo photographers. She was the first woman to be assigned to shoot the National Finals, in 1982, as a professional photographer.

What Lewis is actually doing in the picture is praying, before he gets on his horse. A lot of them do. It's a very religious bunch.

Many of the guys pump themselves up somehow before they go on: they either hyperventilate, slap themselves on the cheeks hard—and I mean really *hard*—or do jumping exercises. It's to get the surge of adrenaline going. It does strengthen you. Very often, I'll come out of the arena, and I'll be dripping blood from a hand or a shin or something, and I don't have a clue how it happened. It didn't hurt at the time, and I'd been concentrating too hard to pay attention. And I think the same thing is true of the riders. They're apt to cream a leg on the chute gate if it's not open wide, and they have to go ahead and ride, whether their kneecap is hanging over in left field or not.

The adrenaline rush that you get the minute you walk into an arena is phenomenal, anyway—it's wonderful. I always feel ten years younger when I get out of an arena than I do when I go in, no matter how tired I am when I start.

Following pages: **The Butt of Lewis Feild,** taken behind the chutes, Pro Rodeo Cowboys Association, Yuma, Arizona, 1984

Foldout: **Dennis Mann riding Soldier,** Pro Rodeo Cowboys Association, Cave Creek, Arizona, 1983

There is an organization called the Cowpunchers' Reunion, made up of ranch hands of all ages who get together to compete and play during the first weekend in August in northern Arizona. These competitors cannot be current members of the PRCA, and the events are markedly different from those in regular rodeo arenas. When I shot the show in 1983, they were not using bucking chutes. Saddle broncs were held between two mounted men ("snubbers") in the middle of the arena. Fathers held calves while their sons were dropped aboard, to ride as far as they could. It was the epitome of old-time rodeo and friendly competition.

Cowpunchers, Williams, Arizona, 1983

48

Kevin Small and Cotton Eye,
Pro Rodeo Cowboys Association,
Tucson, Arizona, 1989

Left: **Billy Neal,** Arizona Rodeo
Association, Sonoita, Arizona, 1963

Page 52: **John Welsh on Little
Britches,** Pro Rodeo Cowboys
Association, Scottsdale, Arizona, 1984

Page 53: **Danny O'Haco,** Pro Rodeo
Cowboys Association bareback rider,
Tucson, Arizona, 1981

Left: **Deb Greenough** adjusting his bareback rigging before riding, Pro Rodeo Cowboys Association, 1993. Deb competed in four rodeos that weekend, on his way to becoming Bareback Champion of the World, Prescott, Arizona, 1993

There is an image that the guys are supposed to have: long sleeves with a hat, properly clean. It's like any sports uniform. You can't compete in the arena in a T-shirt or baseball cap. In the photo called *Hindsight*, they're lined up, watching during slack. There will be a short sleeve or two in there, but that's a no-no in the arena.

We used to call Charlie Sampson "Pee-Wee." In 1982, he "won the world," as we say. He's still riding, but just announced his retirement. He will teach, produce, and promote the new big "bull-oramas," or bull-riding con-tests. He's not that old, but with bull-riders, because of injuries, the life in the arena is a little bit shorter. Most bull-riders don't ride too far into their thirties.

Now he is *Charles* Sampson. There is no more "Pee-Wee"; he's not even "Charlie." He is Charles. For years he used to call me "Lucille." Finally at Calgary I said, "I'll make you a deal. If you'll call me Louise, I'll call you Charles." We've been friends for a long time. He has a great heart.

Chuck Henson is one of my favorite human beings—he's the middle generation of three that I have known and photographed. His mother and his aunt were the "Greenough Girls," as we called them. Alice and Marge came from Montana. In the twenties and thirties, both of these women rode broncs, and they're still around.

Chuck is Marge Greenough Henson's son. He has fought bulls for probably thirty years. Chuck and his wife Nancy have two daughters: Nancy Jane and Leigh-Ann, who is marrying Eric Billingsley. Billingsley is a bronc rider, so they will probably spawn all kinds of little bronc riders and barrel racers. Chuck has finally "retired"— which he's done as many times as I have!

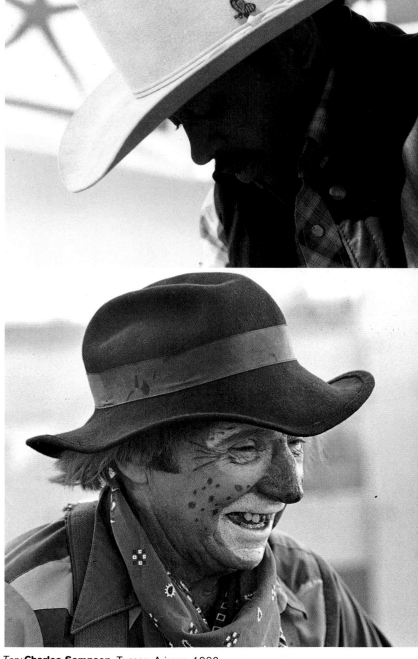

Top: **Charles Sampson,** Tucson, Arizona, 1982
Bottom: **Chuck Henson,** pro-rodeo clown for thirty years, Sonoita, Arizona, 1989

Left: **Eric Billingsley** "blowing out" of the chute on his saddle bronc, Sonoita, Arizona, 1993

Above: **Ivan Daines** on Lynn Beutler's saddle bronc Descent, voted Horse of the Year, Pro Rodeo Cowboys Association, Tucson, Arizona, 1969

The saddle bronc named Descent was the Top Bucking Horse of the Year from 1966 to 1969, and then again in 1971 and 1972. He belonged to the contractors Lynn and Jake Beutler and Mike Cervi. He was just unbelievable—really hard to ride. As you can see in the shot of Ivan Daines on Descent, the rider's out of sync: the horse is coming down, so his feet should be forward, his weight in the stirrups, toes pointed out. Instead, he's gotten caught with his legs behind him, so he's just gripping on for all he's worth. Fortunately, he has the right amount of buck rein to hold, so he's all right. He just needs to get back in rhythm with the horse. Sometimes, horses will drop a shoulder and really throw it at you, so they don't leave you anything to work with or anything to sit on, and then they'll just slam you into the ground.

Here, you can see that Dan Freeman is really using his horse. He happens to be a right-handed rider; so if any part of his left hand touches any part of the horse, that's an automatic disqualification.

Chuck Shepherd, the judge who's standing right behind the horse, is one of the all-time greats. Now in his eighties, he still goes out team-roping. Formerly, when riders were either hurt or healing, they were very apt to judge rodeos. Now judges have to go to clinics, which is great, because there are a lot of new rules and it's much more complicated than it used to be. Today's judges are purely professional—not competing themselves.

Guys wait behind the chutes for their particular event to come up. In *Waiting Room*, they're having quite a "gab fest." This is a good shot of the "pummel," or front of the saddle—an association saddle—without the horn. Also, the stirrup: it's not a wide stirrup like most Western saddles have. The riders sit on their rig on the ground and get it loosened up, get their stirrup leathers working freely, the way they want it to. It's so important to get the right rhythm when you're riding.

Deb Greenough, the current Bareback Champion of the World, has bolts and leather pads, so he can tighten and loosen the handle depending on the weather—the leather is affected, and needs to be adjusted according to the heat or cold, dryness or humidity.

Right: **Dan Freeman,** University of Arizona's National Intercollegiate Rodeo Association, Tucson, Arizona, 1965

Following pages: **Waiting Room,** behind the chutes, Calgary, Alberta, Canada, 1983

Jack Milligan, Arizona Rodeo
Association, Casa Grande,
Arizona, 1964

John Shea here is in trouble, because his toe is behind the bull's elbow, which is not a good place to have it. That means you are getting a little desperate. Ideally, you should keep your toes turned out as hard as you can, with your heels driven into the side. Keeping the toes out helps tense up the groin muscle.

The bulls weigh a ton. I've had one on my chest, so I know. He stepped right on me and split my sternum and two top ribs. What happened was, I tried to get up a fence to get away from him. The guy was still riding him when he got to me—there was no room on the fence. It was full of healthy cowboys, but they weren't expecting me to climb. I thought I'd be able to get out, but I couldn't. The bull came and picked me up by the butt and threw me up in the air. That didn't hurt me at all—I thought, "Oh, is that all there is to it?" But I had a new Leica at that point—only one camera, and it was very expensive—so I was terrified he was going to get the camera. So I sort of curled around the camera in midair. It was when I came down on the ground that the bull really started to go at me. I never did find out where the clown was. He was the one who should have been there to do something. In any event, it got bad enough so the bull horned me right into the ground. Finally, two of my bareback-rider friends threw themselves off the fence and got the bull away from me by distracting him, then pulled me out of the arena like a plug out of a bottle, and dusted me off and set me on my feet. And the announcer said, "Did you get his picture, Louise, or should we run him through again?" I had, in fact, gotten his picture—not a very exciting picture—but one showing that the bull was dead-earnest, and coming right at me.

That was my first trial by fire. And it was good. The one thing I knew I could not do, being the first woman photographer permitted in a rodeo arena, was cry or act afraid or injured or anything else. I had to do like the guys did, or I wasn't going to be allowed back in an arena. So I finished shooting that night. I had no idea how badly I was hurt. I knew it was hard to get my breath—but that was all.

After I finished the rodeo that night, I went to the hospital, because I thought, "Well, it *is* getting a little tough to breathe, I'd better check it out." And they x-rayed me, and said, "The sternum is split and you've broken these little-bitty ribs up here." Of course, the sternum is just cartilage, and what they like to do is tape up your chest. My female anatomy complicated the procedure and confused the doctor. Anyway, they managed to get some kind of tape across my back, in a kind of figure-eight, to keep my shoulders back, so it wouldn't grate. When I got home, and for about two months afterwards, I couldn't do any work in front of me with both hands together. I had to raise the enlarger, focus it with one hand, and then turn around to work. But I'll never forget that doctor scratching his head trying to figure out how the hell to tape me!

John Shea riding Alsbaugh's bull McKinley, Pro Rodeo Cowboys Association, Globe, Arizona, 1985

Above: **Jeff Kobza** taking the bull Sinbad away from Jerry Beagley (on ground), after Beagley had marked a good seventy-six points and fallen on dismount, Pro Rodeo Cowboys Association, Yuma, Arizona, 1983
Right: **Jeff Kobza** misgauging a jump over a bull, Pro Rodeo Cowboys Association, Buckeye, Arizona, 1984

Rodeo clowns are lifesavers; they are not just out there to be funny men. Jumping the bull was popular in the eighties, but isn't done much anymore. It's a tough stunt. The clown can either run and jump off the barrel over a bull, or attempt to do it from the ground. In this particular instance, Jeff Kobza, the clown, misgauged a little, and the bull turned his head just at the wrong time. So it's a picture of him getting reamed out. He was okay, though— sore, but all right.

There has to be total trust in those rodeo clowns. The ones who go to the National Finals (where there are two clowns on the ground and one in a barrel) are picked by the cowboys. They are the ones the riders would most like their lives to be entrusted to. It's the same with the pick-up men, who are every bit as important as the clowns. If a guy gets in trouble on a bucking horse, they are the ones who ride out and pick him off the horse, or get him unhung if he's hung to a stirrup.

These guys really earn respect and trust. And that's the main compensation for the work they do! I mean, they don't make a huge amount of money for a performance. You could never pay enough for what they do.

Above: **Duke Haley,** off the bull, Arizona Rodeo Association, Sierra Vista, Arizona, 1963
Left: **Buck Crofts and dog,** Arizona Rodeo Association, Sierra Vista, Arizona, 1966

Brian Davis "hung up" to his rope,
as Skip Beeler, apprentice bullfighter,
attempts to distract bull, High School
Rodeo Finals, Tucson, Arizona, 1979

Above: **David Fournier** winning the Tucson rodeo on Beutler's bull, Pro Rodeo Cowboys Association, Tucson, Arizona, 1989

Right: **Glen Adair,** Arizona Rodeo Association, Sonoita, Arizona, 1964

It's a wonderful leveler, rodeo. Malcolm Baldridge—who was the U.S. Secretary of Commerce—was a friend of mine. Mac's favorite way of getting rid of the tensions of government was to come out and team rope whenever he could get away. So we had the Secretary of Commerce, out in the arena, in the mud, everybody kidding the devil out of him, because he wasn't as swift as a lot of the other people—he wasn't able to practice as much (although he had a place in Connecticut where he used to rope quite a lot). Sadly, Mac died of a heart attack while roping in the arena. But he died doing what he liked better than anything else in the world—roping with cowboys. He just adored that camaraderie. Nobody will let you take yourself too seriously in rodeo. Nobody expects special treatment.

There used to be prison rodeos. They didn't have roping stock in the state penitentiary, but they imported rough stock. It was a significant leveler for them too: big cell-block bullies—who in normal prison-life would just beat up on the smaller men—would get out there full of bravado, and as often as not, they would get flattened during the first two jumps. Rodeo's a bluff-caller—it's wonderful in that way: you can't cheat at it. If you're good, it will show. If you're not, forget it—move on to something else.

Glen Adair was always in and out of trouble. He was "Peck's Bad Boy," and he would end up in the state pen periodically for short stays. And one of his ways of keeping in touch with the outside world, and particularly with rodeo, was this: every year over Thanksgiving weekend, we would have what is called the Florence Junior Parada, a junior rodeo—in fact, it's the oldest junior rodeo ever. The state pen, which is in the same town, sends a band to play instruments as background for the rodeo—the band's name is "Stars Behind Bars." So you have some totally tone-deaf guys that get into the band on purpose so they can be let out to come play at the rodeo on that weekend. And Glen somehow always managed to get into Stars Behind Bars, so he could come say hi.

Bulls are very agile. You can't outrun a bull. But if you just take a deep breath, and realize that the bull can't turn as fast as you can, then you have more control. So if a bull is coming at you, you wait until he's almost on top of you, and then you step aside or move forward past him.

The only time I ever put that theory to the test, I had absolutely no control over it at all. I'd like to say I was brave. The bull charged the turnback fence, which I was lying under, shooting up into the bullring. It actually charged Chuck Henson, the clown, and caught him around the back at the waist, bruising his kidneys. The bull mashed him into the fence with such force that the fence broke, and it was held up in place by a two-by-six and a base. The two-by-six broke and fell on my head. So there I was, lying on the ground with this fence on top of me. The bull went across the fence, and then turned around and came back at me. I didn't have a prayer, because I was practically out cold, down on the ground. So I waited until the last minute, and then just flipped over, and by that time, they had gotten a rope on the bull and got him away.

One of the judges, Jack Buschbom, came back in the office afterwards. I was sitting with a big banana-shaped bump on the side of my head from this thing, and he said, "That was pretty cool"—to be able to lie there and just move at the last minute. I said, "Cool? I was out cold!"

After that first bull got me—the one that hurt me in the ribs—it took me about a year before I could hold my ground. I'd be gone after one exposure—up a fence, a telephone pole, a tree—anything I could find to get up, without even knowing how I got there. It took me a long time to get over that. I was being a coward, basically!

Apprentice bullfighter Skip Beeler
distracting a bull from the fallen
Andrew Lee and being tossed for his
effort, High School Rodeo Finals,
Chandler, Arizona, 1967

Above: **Conel Thurman** gets a mark
of seventy-three on the bareback
horse Sirocco, Pro Rodeo Cowboys
Association, Cave Creek, Arizona,
1984

Right: **John Clementi riding Pace,**
Turquoise Circuit Finals, Phoenix,
Arizona, 1985

I was a pretty good athlete, and my reflexes aren't
bad. Also, I didn't realize how much body English I put
into shooting, getting down or getting in the right position
or being able to move fast, until last winter, when I couldn't
with my bad knee. It drove me bonkers. I couldn't get down
or kneel to do certain things. (I've since had the knee
"scoped," and it's doing fine.)

Part of it is age and part of it is just being whacked.

You always have adrenaline. Anybody who says he's
not afraid is not going to be a good rider. If you're not a
little bit afraid, you have no business being there. It's
partly respect for the animal, and also for what you're
doing. And it's healthy. It's just like being on stage—like
stage fright. I don't think there is any really good actor or
actress in the world who doesn't have some stage fright.
They say that is what gives them the edge, the last impetus.
You're comfortable once you get into it. But ahead of
time, you're always just a little bit nerved up.

NOTES ON RODEO

Occasioned by the Arena Photography of Louise L. Serpa

by LARRY McMURTRY

1 The visual appeal of rodeo is balletic—but it is a ballet of inadvertence. The bulls, the broncs, the cowboys, have no Balanchine. Their most intricate pas de deux rarely last longer than eight seconds, the time the rider has to stay on the bronc or the bull for the ride to count.

2 These movements are nowhere better captured than in the arena photography of Louise Serpa. Because her bucking photographs are—at one level—motion studies, she has been compared to Muybridge. A better comparison would be to Lotte Jacobi, the great dance-photographer. In rodeo the best sight lines belong to the bucking judges, the arena photographers, the clowns, and the gate hands. All are working professionals, positioned on the arena floor not far from the bucking chutes, where the pas de deux begins (and, often, ends).

3 The ballet of rodeo stems from the quadruped's natural desire to rid itself of whatever is on its back. The unwanted rider might be a rodeo cowboy, but, then again, it might be a cougar, or even a bear. If it's a cowboy, eight seconds is tolerable, but, if it were a bear, eight seconds is much too long—terminal, in fact.

4 Ms. Serpa began in the 1960s, photographing junior rodeo: grade-school cowhands riding milk-pen calves. Proud parents paid her seventy-five cents for her prints. She then went on to high-school and college rodeo—larger cowhands, riding larger stock—amateur rodeo (the sport's wildest, least circumscribed mode), and finally the pros. In 1962 she secured the card that allows her to photograph professional rodeo events from within the arena, and she is at it still, while not neglecting China, Australia, the lovely high plains, or anything else that catches her eclectic eye.

5 To my less eclectic eye, Ms. Serpa's bucking photographs are her most remarkable. Many of them are top-of-the-leap photographs, moments of aerobic extremity. Often she has caught the drama of the ride at the point of denouement, just as gravity is about to recall rider, horse, or bull.

6 In these photographs of the bucking events we travel as far as aesthetics can take us in the rodeo arena. Ms. Serpa is also devoted to the roping events, but here the striving is less extreme, and the visual stakes not quite as high.

7 The bucking events yield Louise Serpa her greatest pictures, but she has not neglected portraiture, or the milieu of rodeo itself, as witnessed in hundreds of arenas, large and small, across the American West. Her work, not so much in as in-and-around the arena, documents a subculture, one about which the sociologists might have more to say than do the aestheticians.

8 I have written of this subculture before, in a small book called *It's Always We Rambled*, known to very few. I don't admire rodeo, whereas Ms. Serpa loves it. Woody Allen recently pointed out that the heart wants what it wants, *i.e.*, one should not be criticized for loving what one loves, even if it happens to be one's wife's adopted child.

9 Ms. Serpa loves rodeo, and I don't like it. Rather than falling back on the appropriate adage—*de gustibus non disputandum est*—a few speculations on our differing perspectives might be in order.

10 First, a little history. Goetzmann's brilliant book *The West of the Imagination* makes clear how instantaneously western experience was packaged for eastern consumers. The artists went in lockstep with the explorers. Rodeo as we know it is an extension of the Wild West show, and Wild West shows were popular well before the West was finally won (or lost, as the revisionists would have it). Buffalo Bill Cody left a Wild West show to go back and help avenge Custer's defeat at the Little Bighorn.

11 In this century rodeo developed a more local mode: the ranch contests, or amateur rodeo. (There still are ranch contests, in which teams of cowhands from local ranches compete against one another in selected events.) Instead of the performers of the famous 101 Ranch touring the world—rodeo's version of the Harlem Globetrotters—cowboys in the vicinity of, say, Wolf, Wyoming would compete against one another for a few days, often in events much wilder than those the schematized, structured world of professional rodeo can admit. Wild-cow milking is a mild example. Steer roping Old Style (now mostly outlawed) is another. In this event one roper and one horse must trip, throw, and tie a full-grown steer; the tripping is the dangerous part, and is as likely to hurt the rider or the horse as it is the steer. Double-mugging, a sedate version involving two ropers to one steer, is the worst you'll see in the pros.

12 Now, rodeo is show biz—its relation to ranch work is oblique at best, and, as ranch work becomes ever more high-tech, the distance grows and the stylized, anachronistic nature of the events is ever more starkly exhibited.

13 Ranch work is, for one thing, communal. One-on-one contests between man and beast are not as common as they once were. Broncs are still broken, and calves are still roped, but throughout the West, both skills are in decline.

14 Buffalo Bill was derided by some "real" scouts because he was a showman first, and only secondarily a "real" scout. So it is with rodeo hands and "real" ranch hands, or cowboys. There is some overlap, but not much: each life is too demanding. Some working cowboys could probably make it as rodeo hands, and a few rodeo hands might survive as real cowboys, but not many. The difference is not skill always; frequently it is temperament. My father, a working cattleman all his life, held rodeo hands in some disdain. In his view they were mostly incompetent fuck-ups, lacking the stability and purposefulness that distinguished the true ranch hand. He admired Bob Crosby, the legendary steer roper, and had a kind word for a few cutting horses and the occasional calf roper, but that was about as far as his grace extended.

15 No one on a working ranch would ever have any reason (or desire) to ride a bull, Brahma or otherwise. No one would ever be required to race a horse around three triangularly placed barrels, an activity that quickly ruins the horse for more productive activity. Bull riding and barrel racing are rodeo *kabuki*—their relation to anything that might happen on a ranch is confined to costume.

16 There is no reason, of course, why show biz, or photography, should be strictly or even principally realistic. The photography of the American West, from the beginning, has been cast in the mode of the romantic-pastoral, as was the art that preceded it. If there is one picture that defines this mode it is Ansel Adams's famous *Moonrise: Hernandez, New Mexico*.

17 In one year recently, I was asked to write introductions to eight books of photographs of cowboys or range life. There can hardly be a cowboy, boot, chuck wagon, saddle horse, or branding iron in the whole West that has not been photographed several times, always in the romantic-pastoral mode.

18 In a sense these are photographs of ghosts, or of a ghost-craft. Only the rich can afford to own ranches now, much less work them. The cattle business long ago ceased to be viable, except to those with money, and lots of it.

19 Cowboys, sensing—like gorillas—that their time has passed, cling ever more desperately to anachronistic styles, not willing to admit that the myth has degenerated, the traditions eroded to a point where attempting to sustain them falls somewhere between silliness and the outright ridiculous.

20 That a craft is dying is sad; not to admit that it is dying, and that, in dying, it approaches parody (as all crafts are apt to) is sadder still. Witness the famous fourth-generation Montana rancher Wally McCrae, who has been, for many years, a principal model for the Marlboro ads. Wally McCrae and some of his peers still insist on dragging calves to the branding fire, rather than using a squeeze-chute. The Montanans can indulge in this stylistic nicety because the money comes from elsewhere, not from selling the calves thus dragged. On our small (but working) ranch in Texas we had a squeeze-chute in 1939.

21 The heart selects—so does the eye. Buffalo Bill (and a few others) invented the dude ranch, an invention whose profound effect on high-plains ranching has yet to be properly assessed. I'm convinced that half the ranches still left in Wyoming and Montana (particularly) wouldn't exist had it not been that so many high-bred, monied eastern girls revolted against the wimpy, Jamesian East by falling in love with cowboys…and cowboys…and cowboys. Ralph Waldo Emerson's great-granddaughter, Ellen Cotton, came west in 1927 in a Rolls Royce convertible and abides here still, on her ranch near Decker, Montana.

22 By a not dissimilar route Louise Serpa made her way from the Chapin School to the arenas of Calgary, Pendleton, and Cheyenne; and photography is the richer. (So, too, is the West—the eastern girls didn't just bring their money, they also brought their taste. Sheridan, Wyoming, where the Queen of England often comes to shop for thoroughbreds, has one of the finest small-town public libraries in the country, and brings speakers at the level of Susan Sontag or John Updike in to enlighten the locals).

23 Louise Serpa fell in love with her first cowboy at age seventeen—I departed from the only cowboy I ever could care about, my father, at age eighteen. She sees cowboys as noble men—indeed, a few of them are noble. I see them as physically competent but emotionally limited men who are in most cases sexist, chauvinist, xenophobic, quasi-fascistic, and not infrequently dull.

24 In photograph after photograph Louise Serpa romanticizes them; in novel after novel I have attempted the reverse, only to find that people won't have it. Richard Avedon found out the same thing when he published

In The American West, the first photography book ever to show the West that I feel I've lived in most of my life. The people in that book are the people who actually live in the little shacks Ansel Adams's moon is rising over. The western land, without question, is magnificent; it is also, and often, brutal. Most western photography shows the land itself, unmarked; *In The American West* shows how the people were marked by this same harsh land. (Appropriately, Avedon's book appeared just as the revisionist historians were proclaiming the winning of the West both a moral and an economic failure.)

25 The revisionist historians (Patricia Nelson Limerick, Donald Worster, et al.) are right in emphasizing the terrible cost that western settlement often exacted; what they can't quite grasp (as a novelist I'm perhaps better positioned to see it) is that the lies about the West are more powerful than the truth about the West—so much more powerful that, in a sense, lies about the West are the truths about the West—the West, at least, of the imagination.

My gripe about rodeo, as publicly promoted, is that it wants both the lie and the truth: to be both the Wild West, and yet steeped in family values. They want the bull riders and the bronc busters to be not merely notable athletes (which they are) but model family-men as well. Suffice it to say that that dual, conflicted expectation has been defied over and over again by the greatest athletes in every sport. The flack over Michael Jordan's gambling is a recent example. The flare of a Casey Tibbs produces great rodeo; the modest calf-roper who helps his wife with the dishes is one more way of suburbanizing the West.

26 I thought *Lonesome Dove* was antimythic; Malory may have felt the same way about the *Morte D'Arthur*. Readers suck so hard at the old myths that they turn stones into grapes.

27 By concentrating on the balletic, the dance of gravity, Louise Serpa has done the same with rodeo, whose only grace is motion. It is not so much the cowboys or the broncs and bulls that are celebrated in these photographs: what's celebrated is the leaping.

ACKNOWLEDGMENTS

My heartfelt thanks:

—to Gene Pruett and George Williams for having enough faith in my ability (regardless of gender) to give me my original press card as "an official press representative of *Rodeo Sports News*, entitled to enter any part of the rodeo grounds." And to the late Dave Stout, Bill Linderman, and all the old gang at 2929 West 19th Avenue in Denver, the headquarters of the Rodeo Cowboys Association.

—to Bill Crawford, longtime editor of the *Pro Rodeo Sports News*, for his friendship and guidance.

—to the stock contractors: Lynn Beutler; the late Walter Alsbaugh and his wife Alice; and Karen and Harry Vold, for their help and kindness both in and out of the arena.

—to the Tucson Rodeo Committee, which has shown me unfailing support and consideration for thirty-three years—bless them!

—to Jim Shepard—originator, owner, and editor for twenty years of the *All-Around*, a rodeo newspaper covering the Southwest—for keeping me straight on facts with his encyclopedic mind, and for being such a booster.

—to the late Willard Porter, editor of *Hoofs and Horns*, who gave me my first magazine cover in 1963.

—and finally, to the countless hard-core rodeo families who have nurtured and protected me in the arena, bought my photographs, fed me, housed me, teased me, and generally kept me going through three generations. I could not have persevered or survived without you.

Aperture gratefully acknowledges the generous support of H. Peter Kriendler.

The staff at Aperture for Rodeo is:
Michael E. Hoffman, Executive Director / Editor in Chief
Roger Straus III, Publisher / General Manager
Melissa Harris, Editor
Michael Sand, Managing Editor
Diana C. Stoll, Associate Editor
Stevan Baron, Production Director
Sandra Greve, Production Manager
Michael Lorenzini, Editorial Assistant
Maura Shea, Editorial Work-Scholar

This edition published by
Könemann Verlagsgesellschaft mbH
Bonner Str. 126, D-50968 Köln

Production manager: Detlev Schaper
Printed and bound: Mateu Cromo

Printed in Spain

ISBN 3-89508-835-8

Previous pages: **Chuck Logue's rigging,** Tucson, Arizona, 1984
Right: **David Thompson** "blowing out" of the chute on the saddle bronc Big Ed, Pro Rodeo Cowboys Association, Tucson, Arizona, 1973
Following page: **Bull riders' waiting room,** Globe, Arizona, 1984
Front cover: **Matt Martin,** High School Rodeo Finals, Douglas, Arizona, 1974